-en as in pen

Carey Molter

Consulting Editor Monica Marx, M.A./Reading Specialist

ABDO
Publishing Company

Published by SandCastle™, an imprint of ABDO Publishing Company, 4940 Viking Drive, Edina, Minnesota 55435.

Printed in the United States.

Credits
Edited by: Pam Price
Curriculum Coordinator: Nancy Tuminelly
Cover and Interior Design and Production: Mighty Media
Photo Credits: Comstock, Corel, Eyewire Images, PhotoDisc

Library of Congress Cataloging-in-Publication Data

Molter, Carey, 1973-
    -En as in pen / Carey Molter.
      p. cm. -- (Word families. Set II)
    Summary: Introduces, in brief text and illustrations, the use of the letter combination "en" in such words as "pen," "seven," "then," and "wren."
    ISBN 1-59197-229-9
    1. Readers (Primary) [1. Vocabulary. 2. Reading.] I. Title. II. Series.

PE1119 .M596 2003
428.1--dc21
                                                2002038628

SandCastle™ books are created by a professional team of educators, reading specialists, and content developers around five essential components that include phonemic awareness, phonics, vocabulary, text comprehension, and fluency. All books are written, reviewed, and leveled for guided reading, early intervention reading, and Accelerated Reader® programs and designed for use in shared, guided, and independent reading and writing activities to support a balanced approach to literacy instruction.

Let Us Know

After reading the book, SandCastle would like you to tell us your stories about reading. What is your favorite page? Was there something hard that you needed help with? Share the ups and downs of learning to read. We want to hear from you! To get posted on the ABDO Publishing Company Web site, send us e-mail at:

sandcastle@abdopub.com

SandCastle Level: Beginning

-en Words

den

men

seven

ten

women

wren

Foxes live in a den.

The men are friends.

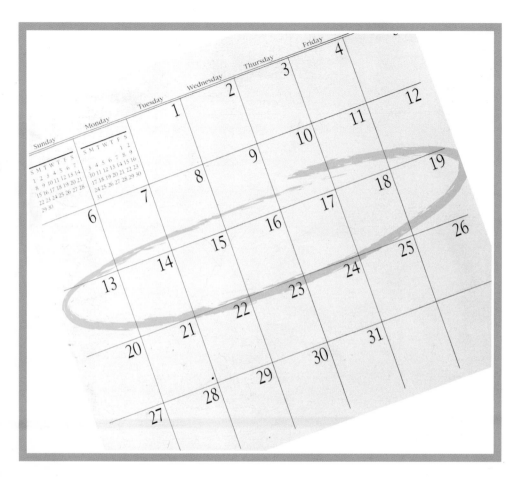

There are seven days in a week.

Ben is ten years old today.

The women are sisters.

A wren is a bird.

Jen the Hen

Jen is a hen.

Jen lives on a farm
owned by Ken.

So does her friend
the wren.

Jen visits the cows
in their pen.

There are ten
in the pen.

Then she visits the fox
near his den.

His name is Ben.

He likes Jen!

Jen visits the sheep
in the glen.

There are seven
in the glen.

When Jen gets tired,
she takes ten.

That Jen,
what a busy hen!

The -en Word Family

Ben	seven
den	ten
glen	then
hen	when
Jen	women
Ken	wren
men	yen
pen	

Glossary

Some of the words in this list may have more than one meaning. The meaning listed here reflects the way the word is used in the book.

den   a small hollow used by an animal for shelter

glen   a small, remote valley

hen   a female bird

pen   a small, fenced area used to hold animals

wren   a small, brown songbird

About SandCastle™

A professional team of educators, reading specialists, and content developers created the SandCastle™ series to support young readers as they develop reading skills and strategies and increase their general knowledge. The SandCastle™ series has four levels that correspond to early literacy development in young children. The levels are provided to help teachers and parents select the appropriate books for young readers.

Emerging Readers
(no flags)

Beginning Readers
(1 flag)

Transitional Readers
(2 flags)

Fluent Readers
(3 flags)

These levels are meant only as a guide. All levels are subject to change.

To see a complete list of SandCastle™ books and other nonfiction titles from ABDO Publishing Company, visit www.abdopub.com or contact us at:

4940 Viking Drive, Edina, Minnesota 55435 • 1-800-800-1312 • fax: 1-952-831-1632